Mason Jar Meals

Delicious and Easy Jar Salads, Jar Lunches,
and More for Meals on the Go

Mason Jar Meals

Delicious and Easy Jar Salads, Jar Lunches,
and More for Meals on the Go

DYLANNA PRESS

Table of Contents

Hot Dishes   **73**

Desserts 81

Beverages 105

Dressings 121

Introduction

MASON JAR MEALS are a fun and practical way to take your meals on the go. When I first discovered the idea of putting salads in Mason jars, I was thrilled. Tired of takeout food, yet not wanting to eat wilted salads for lunch every day, they seemed like the perfect idea.

Inspired from photos on Pinterest, I started experimenting and soon had created and adapted many delicious salad recipes for Mason jars. Next, I turned to breakfast. Wouldn't it be wonderful to wake up in the morning and have breakfast already prepared, just grab and eat? Well it turns out Mason jars work for that, too. Yogurt parfaits, oatmeal, even bacon and eggs, can all be done in these versatile glass jars. And, of course, dinner and dessert ideas work equally well.

Mason jars are an easy way to prepare individual servings, so whether you're cooking for one, two, or a whole crowd, these fun, make-ahead meals will work.

In this book, you'll find a wide variety of recipes including all kinds of salads, as well as hot meal ideas such as mini chicken pot pies and lasagna in a jar. Also included are mouth-watering desserts such as strawberry shortcake, apple pie, and s'mores. To top it off, we've included some refreshing drinks, cocktails, and even a smoothie you can blend right in the jar.

The recipes are easy to prepare and don't require any special cooking skills. So what are you waiting for? Grab your Mason jars and start preparing these gorgeous and tasty dishes!

Why Mason Jars?

YOU MIGHT BE WONDERING, what is the point of making these meals in Mason jars? Why not just use a plastic container? Well, there are a couple of reasons. The first is that Mason jars are a great shape for storing salads. I have not been able to find any plastic containers that equal their layering ability. When you place your dressing in the bottom of the jar and pack a few hardy vegetables on top, the lettuce and other more tender ingredients stay out of the oil and crisper much longer. Which brings me to the second reason—freshness.

Mason jars keep the salads and other recipes fresher longer. I've been able to store these recipes in the refrigerator for up to a week and they still taste fresh. With a typical plastic container, the lettuce is usually wilted the next day. Maybe this is because they are made of glass, or maybe it is due to the tight seal on the jar. Whatever the reason, these salads stay fresher a lot longer. This means that you could whip up a whole batch of Mason jar meals on a Sunday and have your lunches all set for the whole week!

Another advantage is durability. Mason jars are dishwasher safe and are meant to last. Unlike cheap plastic containers that get thrown away after a few uses, these jars can be used again and again.

Safety is another issue. Glass, unlike plastic, will not leak any toxic residues into your food. This is especially important if you need to microwave the dish to reheat it. And, since glass doesn't hold any residues, your salad won't pick up any funky odors. Finally, they just have visual appeal. The clear glass shows off the colorful ingredients in the salads and they look so pretty you might not want to ruin them by eating them!

What Size Jars?

The size of the jar you choose depends on what you are going to put in it. Most of the salad recipes are based on using a quart-size jar. This is because leafy greens take up a lot of room and you don't want to crush them. For some of the other types of recipes, such as yogurt parfaits, desserts, or oatmeal, smaller pint-size and half-pint jars are used. Unless otherwise specified in the recipe, use a quart-size jar. Of course, you are free to adapt this based on your own needs.

When purchasing, look for the wide-mouth jars. This type is a lot easier to fill and eat from.

Where Can I Get Mason Jars?

Some people have told me that they have trouble locating the Mason jars. Personally, I have not found this to be the case and I have seen them everywhere from my local supermarket to Target and Wal-Mart. However, if you can't find them locally, then you can purchase them from Amazon. They have all sizes and types available.

Mason Jar Tutorial

THIS CHAPTER GIVES an overview of the process for making the Mason jar meals. It's pretty simple, but there are a few key points to remember if you want your salads to stay fresh and crisp.

It's All in the Layers

How you layer the ingredients in the jars is the key to making these salads. The order is very important because you need to keep the lettuce and other tender greens away from the dressing so they don't wilt.

Layer One: Dressing

The first layer, at the bottom of the jar, is the dressing. The amount you use really depends on your own personal preference. For most of the recipes, I have recommended 2 tablespoons of dressing, but you can certainly use more or less. I have found that vinaigrette-type dressings are easier to pour out of the jar. The thicker, creamier dressings may have to be scooped out with a spoon.

I've included recipes for various types of dressings. However, if you prefer, bottled dressings will work just as well.

Layer Two: Sturdy Vegetables

The next layer is where you put the ingredients that can stand up to being in the dressing without wilting. This is also where you would place ingredients that you want to marinate. This layer is important because it shields the other, more tender, ingredients from getting soaked in the dressing.

Layer Three: Tender Veggies and Beans

This is the layer you add things like chickpeas, green beans, corn, black beans, avocado, and so on. These are ingredients that are not quite as sturdy as those in the previous layer, but it's okay if they get a little dressing on them.

Layer Four: Pasta, Rice, and Grains

After you've added your veggies, it's time to add the pasta, rice, quinoa, or other grains you might be using. This layer should be pretty well shielded from the dressing.

Layer Five: Meats and Cheese

Now comes the protein layer. Here is where you would add the chicken, tuna, turkey, shrimp, eggs, shredded cheese, feta, etc.

Layer Six: Greens and Toppings

The final layer is where the most delicate ingredients go, such as lettuce, spinach, and other greens, as well as nuts, seeds, and croutons. These are the types of things that would absorb dressing and become soggy after a short time. Sometimes, if I know I'm not going to be eating the salad for several days, I will place the nuts or croutons into a little separate container and put it on top to help them stay really crisp.

So there you have it—just layer up your jars in the proper order and your salads should stay fresh for several days and even up to a week, depending upon the specific ingredients. Of course, not every salad is going to have all six layers, and you may want to adapt any recipe according to your own tastes.

Tips and Tricks

THROUGH TRIAL AND ERROR, I have learned some useful tricks for making Mason jar meals. So in order to save you some time and energy, here are a few things to keep in mind when preparing your meals.

Keeping avocado, apples, etc. from turning brown. If you've ever sliced an apple or avocado and let it sit for a while, you've probably noticed that it turns brown pretty quickly. This makes for a rather unappetizing looking salad. Tossing with lime or other citrus works reasonably well, but is far from perfect. One thing I've found that works is layering red onion next to the avocado. It seems to work due to the sulfur compounds released by the onion. Using this method, I've been able to keep avocado and apple chunks looking good for several days.

Don't overfill the jar. It's tempting to pack as much as you can into the jar to fill it to the top. However, you want to leave a little room at the top so that when you shake it up before eating, there's room for the salad to mix together. If it's packed too tight, nothing will be able to move.

Cool cooked items before placing them in the jars. If you seal hot items into the jars the heat they give off will cause the greens to wilt.

Place croutons, ramen noodles, etc. in separate container or baggie to keep crisp. You can put it inside the jar on top. Doing this will keep them from getting soggy. Make sure your ingredients are dry. Run your greens through a salad spinner and pat down all your veggies with paper towel. If you place wet lettuce into your jar, it is going to get soggy.

Freezing the meals. Some of the recipes are fine to freeze and reheat, such as the mini pot pies, lasagna in a jar, or most of the desserts. However, salads do not do well when frozen.

Part II — Recipes

Breakfast

Make these delicious recipes up the night before and enjoy a quick and healthy breakfast that can be taken on the go.

Strawberry Yogurt Parfait

This is a tasty and healthy way to start the day.

Servings: 4 pint-size jars

Ingredients

2 cups Greek-style plain or vanilla yogurt

2 cups fresh strawberries, sliced

3 cups granola

4 tablespoon cacao nibs (optional)

4 tablespoon slivered almonds (optional)

Directions

Divide ingredients evenly between the jars. Spoon yogurt into jars for bottom layer.

Next, add strawberries and then granola. Top with almonds and cacao nibs.

Seal jar and refrigerate until ready to eat.

Can be eaten straight from the jar or scooped out into bowl.

Coconut-Vanilla Chia Seed Pudding

Chia seeds are packed with nutrients and will keep you satisfied until lunch.

Servings: 1 pint-size jar

Ingredients

1 1/2 cups vanilla coconut milk

1/2 cup chia seeds

1 teaspoon vanilla extract

1 teaspoon honey

Optional ingredients: Your choice of fruit or nuts for topping. Some good choices include blueberries, raspberries, strawberries, slivered almonds, and walnuts.

Directions

Add coconut milk, chia seeds, vanilla, and honey to jar. Close jar and shake well to mix.

Add fresh fruit and nuts if using. Refrigerate for at least 2 hours or overnight.

Shake well before eating.

Apple-Cinnamon Refrigerator Oatmeal

Refrigerator oatmeal is so simple to make and so yummy to eat.

Servings: 4 pint-size jars

Ingredients

2 cups rolled oats (old-fashioned style, not instant)

2 2/3 cups milks (2/3 for each jar)

2 cups Greek-style yogurt

4 tablespoons chia seeds

4 teaspoons cinnamon

2 cups applesauce

4 teaspoons maple syrup

1 cup apples, peeled and chopped

Directions

Divide all ingredients evenly between the jars. Add all ingredients except for apples, seal jars, and shake well to combine. Open jar and add apple chunks to top. Reseal and place in refrigerator overnight.

When ready to eat, open jar and stir to mix in apples.

Will last in refrigerator 2-3 days.

Bacon and Eggs in a Jar

Bacon and eggs cook surprisingly well in a Mason jar.

Servings: 1 pint-size jar

Ingredients

2 large eggs

2 tablespoons milk

2 slices bacon, cooked

Salt and pepper to taste

Optional additions: shredded cheese, spinach, sautéed onions or peppers, or whatever else you like mixed in with your eggs.

Directions

Mix together eggs, milks, salt, pepper, and whatever optional ingredients you've chosen to add.

Pour mixture into Mason jar and microwave for 1-1/2 minutes or until eggs are cooked. Be sure lid is not on Mason jar when you microwave.

Crumble bacon on top of eggs and enjoy!

Note: This meal is best eaten right away once cooked but you can store the mixture in the refrigerator uncooked and then just pop in the microwave when ready to eat.

Blueberry-Maple Refrigerator Oatmeal

■ ● ■ ■ ● ■ ■ ● ■ ● ■ ● ■ ● ■ ● ■ ■

This another of my favorite oatmeal flavor combinations.

Servings: 4 pint-size jars

Ingredients

2 cups rolled oats (old-fashioned style, not instant)

2 2/3 cups milks (2/3 for each jar)

2 cups Greek-style yogurt

4 tablespoons chia seeds

4 tablespoons maple syrup

2 cups fresh blueberries

Directions

Divide all ingredients evenly between the jars. Add all ingredients and shake well to combine. Place in refrigerator overnight.

Will last in refrigerator 2-3 days.

Salads

● ■ ■ ■ ■ ● ■ ■ ■ ● ■ ■ ■ ● ■ ■

The possibilities for salads in a jar are virtually endless. Almost any traditional salad can be adapted to a Mason jar, making for a healthy, crunchy lunch you can take with you. These salads stay fresh for up to 5 or 6 days in the refrigerator, so make up a batch ahead of time and you won't have to order a fast food lunch all week!

Veggie Pasta Salad

This is one of my favorite on-the-go lunches.

Servings: 4 jars

Ingredients

1/2 cup Caesar Vinaigrette Dressing

1 bunch asparagus, cut in 2-inch pieces

1 cup red bell pepper, chopped

1 cup mushrooms, sliced

1 cup red onion, chopped

4 cups spiral pasta, cooked

15-20 kalamata olives, pitted and halved

4 ounce feta cheese, crumbled

4 tablespoon walnuts, chopped

Directions

Steam asparagus until just tender (about 1-2 minutes). Rinse immediately in cold water and cut into pieces.

Divide dressing evenly and pour into jars. Layer in asparagus, bell pepper, mushrooms, and red onion, dividing evenly between jars.

Next, add spiral pasta. Top with olives, feta cheese, and walnuts.

Seal jars and store in refrigerator until ready to eat.

Before serving, shake jar a few times to mix dressing. Pour into bowl or eat right from the jar.

Taco Salad

This quick taco salad is delicious. Add jalapenos for added kick.

Servings: 4 jars

Ingredients

12 ounces ground beef

1 packet taco seasoning mix

1/3 cup water

1/4 fresh cilantro, chopped

1 cup salsa, homemade or jarred

2 cups tomatoes, chopped

1 small red onion, diced

1 cup red or yellow bell pepper, diced

1 cup jalapenos, chopped (optional)

4 cups romaine lettuce, chopped

1 cup shredded Mexican cheese

Directions

In a large nonstick skillet, brown beef until it is cooked through and no longer pink. Add seasoning packet along with 1/3 cup water and cilantro. Stir together until beef crumbles.

Put 1/4 cup of salsa in the bottom of each jar. Next, divide ingredients into fourths and add to Mason jars in this order: tomatoes, red onion, bell pepper, jalapenos (if using), taco meat, lettuce, and shredded cheese on top.

Seal jars and store in refrigerator until ready to eat.

Pour into bowl to eat. Serve with tortilla chips.

Shake It Up Salad

Don't shake until you're ready to eat it to keep your lettuce crisp.

Servings: 4 jars

Ingredients

1/2 cup Balsamic Vinaigrette Dressing

1 cup grape tomatoes

1 large cucumber, peeled and diced

1/2 red onion, diced

1 cup shredded cheddar cheese

1 head romaine lettuce, washed, rinsed, and coarsely chopped

1/2 cup roasted, unsalted sunflower seeds

Directions

Divide dressing evenly into the jars. Layer remaining ingredients in order into the jars: tomatoes, cucumber, onion, cheese, lettuce, and sunflower seeds.

Seal jar and refrigerate until ready to eat.

To serve, shake jar to coat salad with dressing. Pour into bowl or eat right from the jar.

Rainbow Fruit Salad

This colorful salad is as pretty as it is delicious.

Servings: 4 jars

Ingredients

1/2 cup Sweet Citrus Dressing

1 medium-sized bunch of red grapes

1 cup blueberries

4 kiwis, peeled and sliced

1 nectarine, unpeeled, sliced into triangles

1 large mango, peeled and diced

1 cup strawberries, sliced

Directions

Divide dressing evenly into the four jars.

Divide fruit evenly and layer in jars in this order: grapes, blueberries, kiwis, nectarine, mango, and strawberries.

Seal jar and store in refrigerator until ready to eat.

Shake gently before serving to coat fruit with dressing.

Tomato, Mozzarella, and Basil Salad

This tastes best with ripe tomatoes from the garden or farmer's market and fresh basil.

Servings: 4

Ingredients

1/4 extra-virgin olive oil

1/4 balsamic vinegar

8 plum tomatoes, quartered

4-6 yellow tomatoes, quartered

6 ounces mozzarella cheese, cubed

1/3 cup fresh basil leaves, minced

Salt and ground black pepper to taste

Directions

Whisk together the olive oil, vinegar, salt, and pepper. Pour into jars, 1/4 in each.

Add tomatoes, mozzarella cheese, and basil.

Seal jar and refrigerate until ready to eat.

To serve, shake jar to coat salad with dressing. Pour into bowl or eat right from the jar.

Spinach Blueberry Salad

* ■ ■ ■ ● ■ ■ ■ ■ ● ■ ■ ■ ● ■ ■

*Toasted pecans add just the right amount of crunch to this
super foods combo salad.*

Servings: 4

Ingredients

1/2 cup Raspberry Vinaigrette Dressing

2 cups fresh blueberries

4 ounces blue cheese, crumbled

4 cups fresh baby spinach

1/2 cup pecans, toasted and chopped (could use candied)

Directions

Divide dressing evenly into the jars. Layer remaining **Ingredients** in order into the jars: blueberries, blue cheese, baby spinach, pecans.

Seal jars and refrigerate until ready to eat.

To serve, shake jar to coat salad with dressing. Pour into bowl or eat right from the jar.

Greek Chicken Salad

This delicious and filling salad should saisfy even the heartiest appetite.

Servings: 4 jars

Ingredients

1/2 cup Greek Dressing

1 large tomato, diced

1 medium cucumber, peeled and diced

1/2 red onion, diced

1/2 cup kalamta olives, pitted and sliced

2 cups cooked chicken, diced (leftover, store-bought, or poached)

1/2 cup feta cheese, crumbled

1 head romaine lettuce, coarsely chopped (about 4 cups)

Directions

Divide dressing evenly into the jars. Layer remaining ingredients in order into the jars: tomato, cucumber, red onion, olives, chicken, feta cheese, lettuce.

Seal jar and refrigerate until ready to eat.

To serve, shake jar to coat salad with dressing. Pour into bowl or eat right from the jar.

Greek Salad

This healthy Mediterranean salad is rich with kalamata olives and feta cheese.

Servings: 4 jars

Ingredients

1/2 cup Greek Dressing

1 large tomato, diced

1 medium cucumber, peeled and diced

1 red bell pepper, diced

1/2 red onion, diced

1/2 cup kalamta olives, pitted and sliced

1/2 cup feta cheese, crumbled

1 head romaine lettuce, coarsely chopped (about 4 cups)

Directions

Divide dressing evenly into the jars. Layer remaining ingredients in order into the jars: tomato, cucumber, red pepper, red onion, olives, feta cheese, lettuce.

Seal jars and refrigerate until ready to eat.

To serve, shake jar to coat salad with dressing. Pour into bowl or eat right from the jar.

Beet and Arugula Salad

● ■ ■ ■ ● ■ ■ ■ ● ■ ■ ■ ■ ● ■ ■

The sweetness of the beets contrasts nicely with the slightly bitter arugula.

Servings: 4 jars

Ingredients

1/2 cup Balsamic Vinaigrette

4 beets, greens trimmed

1/2 red onion, sliced

2 bunches arugula, coarsely chopped

4 ounces goat cheese

1/2 cup candied walnuts

Directions

Divide dressing evenly into the jars. Divide and layer remaining ingredients in order into the jars: red onions, beets, goat cheese, arugula, walnuts.

Seal jars and refrigerate until ready to eat.

To serve, shake jar to coat salad with dressing. Pour into bowl or eat right from the jar.

Tortellini Salad in a Jar

This pasta salad is delicious and filling.

Servings: 4 jars

Ingredients

1/2 cup Caesar Vinaigrette Dressing

1 quart grape tomatoes, halved

1 small red onion, diced

1 12-ounce jar artichoke hearts

2 cups cheese tortellini, cooked

4 ounces goat cheese

4 cups baby spinach (could also use a blend of baby greens)

Directions

Pour dressing evenly into each of the four jars. Divide and layer remaining ingredients in order into the jars: tomatoes, onion, artichokes, tortellini, goat cheese, and baby spinach.

Seal jars and refrigerate until ready to eat.

To serve, shake jar to coat salad with dressing. Pour into bowl or eat right from the jar.

California Roll Salad

Servings: 4 jars

Ingredients

2 cups brown rice, cooked

3 tablespoons rice vinegar

3 tablespoon soy sauce

1 cucumber, peeled and diced

1 tablespoon lemon juice

2 avocados, diced

2 nori sheets, cut into pieces

1 pound crab meat or surimi (imitation crab meat)

Directions

In a bowl mix rice vinegar and soy sauce. Add rice and mix to coat.

Put avocado in a bowl and pour lemon juice over avocado and mix gently to coat.

Divide ingredients into equal fourths and then add to jars in this order: rice, cucumber, nori, crab or surimi, and avocado.

Seal jars and refrigerate until ready to eat.

To serve, pour onto a plate or eat right from the jar.

Three-Bean Salad

I love the textures in this tasty salad.

Servings: 4 jars

Ingredients

1/2 cup Balsamic Vinaigrette Dressing

4 cups couscous, cooked

1 large cucumber, peeled and diced

1 red pepper, diced

1 can black beans, drained

1 can cannellini beans, drained

1 can chickpeas, drained

4 ounces feta cheese

1/2 cup fresh cilantro, chopped

Directions

Pour dressing evenly into each of the four jars. Divide and layer remaining ingredients in order into the jars: couscous, cucumber, red pepper, chickpeas, black beans, cannellini beans, feta cheese, and cilantro.

Seal jars and refrigerate until ready to eat.

To serve, shake jar to coat salad with dressing. Pour into bowl or eat right from the jar.

Red Cabbage Slaw

●   ■   ■   ■   ◆   ■   ■   ■   ◆   ■   ■   ■   ◆   ■   ■

This crunch coleslaw looks dazzling in the jar.

Servings: 4 jars
Ingredients
1/2 cup Honey Mustard Vinaigrette
1/2 medium red cabbage, coarsely shredded
1 cup grated carrots
1/2 red onion, diced
3 large red apples, unpeeled, cut into small chunks
1/2 walnuts, finely chopped
parsley, chopped, for garnish

Directions

Pour dressing evenly into each of the four jars. Divide and layer remaining ingredients in order into the jars: cabbage, red onion, grated carrots, apples, walnuts. Sprinkle with parsley for garnish.

Seal jars and refrigerate until ready to eat.

To serve, shake jar to coat salad with dressing. Pour into bowl or eat right from the jar.

Orzo Salad

This fresh and delicious salad is sure to please.

Servings: 4 jars

Ingredients

1/2 cup Balsamic Vinaigrette Dressing

1/2 red onion, chopped

1/2 cup black olives, pitted and sliced

1 red pepper, diced

2 cups baby spinach, chopped

4 cups orzo, cooked

1 cup cooked chicken breast, skinless and cubed

4 ounces feta cheese, crumbled

1/2 cup pine nuts, lightly toasted

Directions

Pour dressing evenly into each of the four jars. Divide and layer remaining ingredients in order into the jars: onion, olives, red pepper, orzo, chicken, feta cheese, spinach, and pine nuts.

Seal jars and refrigerate until ready to eat.

To serve, shake jar to coat salad with dressing. Pour into bowl or eat right from the jar.

Baby Greens Salad
with Nuts and Berries

This summery salad is bursting with berry goodness.

Servings: 4 jars

Ingredients

1/2 cup Raspberry Vinaigrette Dressing

1/2 red onion, chopped

1 cup fresh blueberries

1 cup fresh strawberries, sliced

1 cup blue cheese, crumbled

4 cups mixed baby greens

1 cup silvered almonds

Directions

Pour dressing evenly into each of the four jars. Divide and layer remaining ingredients in order into the jars: onion, blueberries, strawberries, bleu cheese, baby greens, and almonds.

Seal jars and refrigerate until ready to eat.

To serve, shake jar to coat salad with dressing. Pour into bowl or eat right from the jar.

Wild Rice Salad with Kale, Walnuts, and Pomegranate

The ruby red of the pomegranate seeds and the deep green kale make for a very elegant salad.

Servings: 4 jars

Ingredients

1/2 Honey Dijon Dressing

4 cups wild rice, cooked

1 cup pomegranate seeds

4 ounces feta cheese, crumbled

2 cups baby kale, chopped

1/3 cup walnuts, toasted

Directions

Pour dressing evenly into each of the four jars. Divide and layer remaining ingredients in order into the jars: wild rice, pomegranate, feta cheese, kale, and walnuts. Seal jars and refrigerate until ready to eat.

To serve, shake jar to coat salad with dressing. Pour into bowl or eat right from the jar.

Quinoa Salad with Chicken and Walnuts

If you haven't tried quinoa yet, this salad is a great introduction.

Servings: 4 jars

Ingredients

1/2 cup White Wine Vinaigrette Dressing

1/2 red onion, diced

1/2 cup celery, diced

1/2 cup dried cherries

4 cups quinoa, cooked (1 cup uncooked)

1 cup chicken breast, cooked and diced

1/2 cup walnuts, chopped and toasted

Directions

Pour dressing evenly into each of the four jars. Divide and layer remaining ingredients in order into the jars: onion, celery, cherries, quinoa, chicken, and walnuts. Seal jars and refrigerate until ready to eat.

To serve, shake jar to coat salad with dressing. Pour into bowl or eat right from the jar.

Salmon Niçoise Salad

This twist on a classic French staple works well layered in the jar.

Servings: 4 jars

Ingredients

1/ 2 cup Balsamic Vinaigrette Dressing

1 cup grape tomatoes, halved

8 radishes, trimmed and sliced

10 ounces green beans, preferable haricots verts, lightly steamed

1 pound small red potatoes, cooked and quartered

1/2 cup black olives, pitted

4 eggs, hardboiled

12 ounces salmon, cooked (could substitute with canned salmon)

1 head lettuce, Boston or Romaine, coarsely chopped

Directions

Pour dressing evenly into each of the four jars. Divide and layer remaining ingredients in order into the jars: tomatoes, radishes, green beans, potatoes, olives, eggs, salmon, lettuce.

Seal jars and refrigerate until ready to eat.

To serve, shake jar to coat salad with dressing. Pour into bowl or eat right from the jar.

Asian Noodle Salad

* ▪ ▪ ▪ ▪ ▪ ▪ ▪ ▪ ▪ ▪ ▪ ▪ ▪

Red pepper flakes give this noodle salad a little kick.

Servings: 4 jars

Ingredients

1/4 cup rice wine vinegar

1/4 cup soy sauce (low-sodium)

1 teaspoon sesame oil

4 tablespoons extra-virgin olive oil

juice from 1 lime

1 large garlic clove, minced

1 tablespoon sugar

2 teaspoons red pepper flakes

1 cup carrots, shredded

2 celery stalks, diced

1 cup red cabbage, shredded

1/2 red bell pepper, diced

1 package soba noodles, cooked

1/1 cup fresh cilantro, minced

1/2 cup peanuts, roasted and unsalted

Directions

In a bowl, whisk together the rice wine vinegar, soy sauce, sesame oil, olive oil, lime juice, garlic, sugar, and red pepper flakes. Divide this mixture evenly among the 4 jars.

Next, layer the remaining ingredients into the jars in this order: carrots, celery, cabbage, red pepper, soba noodles, cilantro, and peanuts.

Seal jars and refrigerate until ready to eat.

To serve, shake jar to coat salad with dressing. Pour into bowl or eat right from the jar.

Wheat Berry, Apple, and Walnut Salad

Wheat berries are a versatile whole grain with a sweet, nutty taste.

Servings: 4 jars

Ingredients

2 cups wheat berries

8 cups water

1/2 cup extra-virgin olive oil

4 tablespoons lemon juice + 1 teaspoon lemon juice

 1 scallion, chopped

1/3 cup fresh parsley, chopped

Salt and pepper to taste

1/2 cup celery, diced

1/2 cup dried cherries

2 large apples, skin-on, diced

1/2 cup walnuts, chopped and toasted

Directions

Combine water and wheat berries in a large pot. Bring to a boil, reduce heat, and cook wheat berries for 1 hour, or until tender. Drain and let cool.

In a bowl, whisk together olive oil, 4 tablespoons lemon juice, scallion, parsley, salt and pepper. Divide this evenly among the 4 jars.

Put apples in small bowl and toss with remaining 1 teaspoon of lemon juice.

Divide ingredients evenly and layer in jars in this order: celery, cherries, wheat berries, apples, and walnuts.

Seal jars and refrigerate until ready to eat.

To serve, shake jar to coat salad with dressing. Pour into bowl or eat right from the jar.

Cobb Salad

This high-protein salad is perfect for those on a low-carb diet and looks really pretty layered in the jar.

Servings: 4 jars

Ingredients

1/2 cup Honey Mustard Vinaigrette

2 large tomatoes, diced

1 avocado, diced

1/2 pound cooked ham, cubed

1 cup chicken, cooked and diced (leftover, store bought, or poached)

2 eggs, hard-boiled and sliced

4 ounces blue cheese, crumbled

4 cups romaine lettuce, coarsely chopped

2 cups watercress

Directions

Pour dressing evenly between the jars. Divide and layer remaining ingredients in order into the jars: tomatoes, avocado, ham, eggs, chicken, romaine, watercress. Seal jars and refrigerate until ready to eat.

To serve, shake jar to coat salad with dressing. Pour into bowl or eat right from the jar.

Sardine Salad

Sardines are chock-full of healthy omega-3 fatty acids.

Servings: 4 jars

Ingredients

1/2 cup Balsamic Vinaigrette Dressing

2 large tomatoes, cut into chunks

1 small red onion, diced

2 ripe avocados, cut into cubes, without skin

Juice of 1 lemon

2 cans sardines, packed in olive oil

4 ounces feta cheese

4 cups romaine lettuce, coarsely chopped

Directions

In a bowl, toss the avocado with the lemon juice to prevent browning.

Pour dressing evenly into each of the four jars. Divide and layer remaining ingredients in order into the jars: tomatoes, red onion, avocado, sardines, feta cheese, and romaine.

Seal jars and refrigerate until ready to eat.

To serve, shake jar to coat salad with dressing. Pour into bowl or eat right from the jar.

Citrus and Avocado Salad

This summery, light salad is delicious.

Servings: 4 jars

Ingredients

1/2 cup Sweet Citrus Dressing

2 navel oranges, peeled and cut into slices

1 red onion, sliced into rings

2 large avocado, scooped from skin and cubed

4 cups spring mix greens, prewashed

1/2 cup candied pecans

Directions

Pour dressing evenly into each of the four jars. Divide and layer remaining ingredients in order into the jars: red onion, oranges, avocado, greens, and pecans.

Seal jars and refrigerate until ready to eat.

To serve, shake jar to coat salad with dressing. Pour into bowl or eat right from the jar.

Spinach and Mushroom Salad with Sunflower Seeds

The mushrooms are added first in this salad to let them marinate in the dressing.

Servings: 4 jars

Ingredients

1/2 cup Poppy Seed Dressing

1 cup mushrooms, stems removed, sliced

1 quart grape tomatoes

1 cup carrots, shredded

1/2 cup black olives, pitted and sliced

4 cups baby spinach, lightly packed

4 tablespoons sunflower seeds, roasted and unsalted

Directions

Pour dressing evenly into each of the four jars. Divide and layer remaining ingredients in order into the jars: mushrooms, tomatoes, shredded carrots, olives, spinach. Sprinkle sunflower seeds on top.

Seal jars and refrigerate until ready to eat.

Chopped Spinach and Kale Salad with Apples

This powerhouse salad is packed with antioxidants.

Servings: 4 jars

Ingredients

1/2 cup Balsamic Vinaigrette Dressing

2 cups carrots, shredded

1 cup celery, shredded

4 scallions, chopped

2 large apples, cubed, skin on

juice of 1 lemon

1/2 radishes, sliced

1 cup dried cranberries

3 cups kale, coarsely chopped

3 cups spinach, coarsely chopped

1/2 cup walnuts, toasted

Directions

Place apples cubes in a bowl and pour lemon juice over them. Mix to coat.

Pour dressing evenly into each of the four jars. Divide and layer remaining ingredients in order into the jars: carrots, celery, scallions, radishes, apples, cranberries, kale spinach, and walnuts.

Seal jars and refrigerate until ready to eat.

To serve, shake jar to coat salad with dressing. Pour into bowl or eat right from the jar.

Shrimp and Mango Orzo Salad

The flavors of mint and cilantro combine beautifully in this summery salad.

Servings: 4 jars

Ingredients

1/2 cup White Wine Vinaigrette

2 mangoes, peeled, pitted, and sliced

Juice of 2 limes

1/4 cup fresh cilantro, chopped

1/8 cup fresh mint, chopped

1 red pepper, diced

1 15-ounce can black beans, drained

1 pound cooked shrimp, peeled and deveined

2 cups lettuce leaves

Directions

In a bowl, toss together mangoes, cilantro mint, and lime juice.

Pour dressing evenly into each of the four jars. Divide and layer remaining ingredients in order into the jars: red pepper, mango mixture, black beans, shrimp, and lettuce.

Seal jars and refrigerate until ready to eat.

To serve, shake jar to coat salad with dressing. Pour into bowl or eat right from the jar.

Chopped Tuna Salad

This quick and easy salad tastes great.

Servings: 4 jars

Ingredients

1/2 cup Lemon Yogurt Dressing

2 large tomatoes, chopped

1/2 red onion, diced

1 large cucumber, peeled and diced

1 avocado, peeled, pitted, and diced

1/2 cup black olives, pitted and sliced

1 can white tuna in olive oil, drained

2 cups romaine lettuce, coarsely chopped

Directions

Pour dressing evenly into each of the four jars. Divide and layer remaining ingredients in order into the jars: tomatoes, onion, cucumber, olives, avocado, tuna, and romaine.

Seal jars and refrigerate until ready to eat.

To serve, shake jar to coat salad with dressing. Pour into bowl or eat right from the jar.

Buffalo Chicken Salad

This is my husband's all-time-favorite chicken salad recipe. It's like buffalo wings in a jar.

Servings: 4 jars

Ingredients

1 pound chicken tenders

1/2 cup Frank's Red Hot Wings hot sauce (or similar)

2 tablespoons olive oil

1/2 cup blue cheese dressing

1 quart grape tomatoes

1 cup celery, chopped

1/4 cup blue cheese, crumbled

4 cups romaine lettuce, coarsely chopped

Directions

Preheat broiler. Spray broiling pan with nonstick cooking spray. In a bowl, toss chicken with the olive oil and hot sauce until coated. Lay chicken on broiler pan and broil in oven about 5-6 minutes, or until cooked through.

Pour blue cheese dressing evenly into each of the four jars. Divide and layer remaining ingredients in order into the jars: tomatoes, celery, chicken, blue cheese, and romaine lettuce.

Seal jars and refrigerate until ready to eat.

To serve, shake jar to coat salad with dressing. Pour into bowl or eat right from the jar.

Hot Dishes

* ■ ■ ■ ● ■ ■ ■ ● ■ ■ ■ ● ■ ■

Mason jars are not just for salads. They are also perfect for making individual size hot dishes that can be quickly reheated in the microwave or oven.

Chicken and Broccoli Shells

* ▪ ▪ ▪ ● ▪ ▪ ▪ ● ▪ ▪ ▪ ● ▪ ▪

This is one of my favorite dinners. Adapted for the jar, it works great for lunch too.

Servings: 6 pint size jars

Ingredients

4 tablespoons olive oil

3 cloves garlic, minced

1 pound chicken tenderloins, cut into small pieces

2 cups broccoli florets, cut into small pieces

1 box pasta shells

1/2 cup parmesan cheese

Directions

Cook pasta according to package **Directions**.

While pasta is cooking, heat olive oil in a large skillet over medium heat. Add garlic and cook for 2-3 minutes. Add chicken and cook for 2-3 minutes. Add broccoli and continue to cook, stirring occasionally until chicken is cooked through and broccoli is tender.

To each jar, add about a cup of pasta shells, topped with 1/6 of chicken and broccoli mixture. Sprinkle parmesan cheese on top.

Serve and eat while still hot or seal jars and store in refrigerator until ready to eat. Can be eaten later cold or reheated in the microwave (remove lid before placing in microwave). Shake gently before eating.

Lasagna in a Jar

Bubbly, cheesy goodness baked right in the jar.

Servings: 6 8-ounce jars

Ingredients

1 pound lean ground beef

1 clove garlic, minced

1/4 yellow onion, minced

1 tablespoon olive oil

2 cups marinara sauce, homemade or jarred

10 ounces ricotta cheese

1/2 parmesan cheese, grated plus extra for sprinkling on top

1 egg

Salt and pepper to taste

1 cup mozzarella, shredded

1 package no-boil lasagna noodles

Directions

In a large skillet over medium high heat, sauté garlic and onion in olive oil for a 2-3 minutes. Add ground beef and cook until beef is browned all the way through. Drain excess oil.

Break apart lasagna noodles so they fit into the jars (in thirds).

In a bowl, mix together ricotta cheese, egg, parmesan, and salt and pepper.

Place lasagna noodle in bottom of each jar. Add a spoonful or so each of cheese mixture, ground beef, tomato sauce, and mozzarella cheese. Repeat with second layer. Add one more lasagna noodle, a little sauce, and mozzarella cheese. Sprinkle with grated parmesan.

Place jars on cookie sheet. Bake, uncovered, in 350 degree oven for 30-35 minutes or until cheese is golden brown.

May be frozen before or after cooking. To cook from frozen, allow to come to room temperature before heating.

Mini Chicken Pot Pies

These little pot pies are perfect for a hot lunch.

Servings: 4 pint-size jars

Ingredients

4 9-inch pie crusts, premade or store bought

1 pound chicken tenders, cut into small chunks

1/2 yellow onion, chopped

2 cloves garlic, minced

2 tablespoons olive oil

1 1/2 cups chicken gravy, premade or store bought

1 bag frozen mixed vegetables (carrots, peas, and corn)

2 tablespoons butter, melted

Directions

Lay out the pie crust on a floured surface. Use the ring from one of the jars to cut 8 circles out of the dough. Set these aside for the tops.

Line each of the jars with dough. Press firmly against the sides of the jar.

In a large skillet, heat olive oil over medium heat. Add onion and garlic and sauté for 2-3 minutes. Add chicken and cook until chicken is no longer pink, about 5-6 minutes. Add frozen vegetables and gravy and continue to cook for a few more minutes. Divide the chicken mixture evenly and scoop into each of the jars, filling almost to the top. Top with round pie crust cut-out. Pinch edges. Vent top of crust. Brush each top with the melted butter.

Put jars on cookie sheet. Bake in preheated 425 degree oven for 30-40 minutes or until pie crust turns golden brown.

Pies may also be frozen before baking. If baking from frozen, allow jar to come to room temperature before baking.

Spaghetti and Meatballs

* ▪ ▪ ▪ ● ▪ ▪ ▪ ▪ ● ▪ ▪ ▪ ● ▪ ▪

Make these up ahead of time and reheat in the microwave for a quick hot lunch or dinner.

Servings: 4 pint-size jars

Ingredients

1/2 box of spaghetti

2 cups tomato sauce, homemade or jarred

16-20 mini meatballs, homemade or frozen

1/2 cup parmesan cheese, grated

Directions

Cook spaghetti according to package **Directions**

Heat tomato sauce and meatballs in a saucepan over medium heat until sauce is hot and meatballs are heated through.

In each jar layer: spaghetti, 1/2 cup sauce, 4-5 meatballs, and top with grated parmesan cheese.

Serve and eat while still hot or seal jars and store in refrigerator until ready to eat.

Reheat in the microwave (remove lid before placing in microwave). Shake gently before eating.

Desserts

Mason jars are perfect for individual-sized desserts.

Candy Cane Cupcakes

These would make a nice gift or dessert at Christmastime.

Servings: 8 eight-ounce jars

Ingredients

2/3 cup all-purpose flour

1 1/2 tablespoons cocoa powder, unsweetened

3/4 teaspoon baking powder

1/2 teaspoon salt

10 tablespoons butter, melted

3/4 cup sugar

3 large eggs

1 teaspoon vanilla

1 cup vanilla frosting, homemade or prepared

1/2 teaspoon peppermint extract

2-3 drops red food coloring

1/2 peppermint candies, crushed

Directions

Preheat oven to 350 degrees. In a large bowl, mix together flour, cocoa powder, baking powder, and salt. In a separate bowl., mix together butter and sugar. Add in eggs and vanilla and mix until combined. Fold in flour mixture and mix until smooth. Divide mixture evenly between the jars. Place jars on cookies sheet and bake for 22-25 minutes or until toothpick comes out clean. Remove from oven and cool before frosting.

For the frosting: Add peppermint extract to frosting and mix. To get red-and-white striped frosting, draw three vertical lines of food coloring with toothpick inside of piping bag. Fill with frosting; when frosting is squeezed out, stripes will appear. Frost cupcakes in jars and top with a spoonful of crushed candies.

Vanilla Punch Bowl Cake

This layered cake is easy to make and looks pretty, too!

Servings: 8 one-pint jars

Ingredients

1 box yellow cake mix

1 20-ounce can crushed pineapple

2 cups whipped cream (or frozen whipped topping)

2 cups fresh strawberries, sliced

Directions

Make cake according to package **Directions**. Can bake as one sheet or 2 round pans. Allow to cool completely. Cut cake into 1-inch cubes.

Divide ingredients evenly between the jar and layer in this order: cake cubes, a large spoonful of pineapple, a large spoonful of whipped cream, another layer of cake, a large spoonful of strawberries, top with another spoonful of whipped cream.

Seal jars and place in refrigerator for at least several hours before serving.

Strawberry Shortcake

Impress your guests with this super easy to make dessert.

Servings: 8 pint-size jars

Ingredients

1 pre-made or pre-bought pound cake

4 cups strawberries, sliced

2 tablespoons sugar

4 cups whipped cream

Directions

Cut cake into 1-inch cubes.

Put strawberry slices in a bowl and sprinkle with sugar. Stir to coat strawberries.

Layer the ingredients in the jars in this order: cake, strawberries, whipped cream.

Repeat for second layer. Top with a slice of strawberry.

Serve immediately or seal jars and refrigerate until ready to eat.

Brownie Cupcakes in a Jar

These are fudgy and oh so chocolaty good!

Servings: 8 eight-ounce jars

Ingredients

2/3 cup all-purpose flour

1 1/2 tablespoons cocoa powder, unsweetened

3/4 teaspoon baking powder

1/2 teaspoon salt

10 tablespoons butter, melted

3/4 cup sugar

3 large eggs

1 teaspoon vanilla

1 cup chocolate fudge frosting

1/2 cup chocolate chips, bittersweet, dark, or semisweet

Directions

Preheat oven to 350 degrees. In a large bowl, mix together flour, cocoa powder, baking powder, and salt. In a separate bowl., mix together butter and sugar. Add in eggs and vanilla and mix until combined. Fold in flour mixture and mix until smooth. Divide mixture evenly between the jars. Place jars on cookies sheet and bake for 22-25 minutes or until toothpick comes out clean. Remove from oven and cool before frosting.

Frost cupcakes in jars and top with a spoonful of chocolate chips.

S'Mores

These are chocolaty, gooey, and delicious!

Servings: 6 8-ounce jars

Ingredients

1 1/2 cups graham cracker crumbs

1/3 cup sugar

6 tablespoons butter, melted

1 12-ounce bag of milk chocolate chips

3/4 cup heavy cream

1 and 1/2 cups mini marshmallows

Directions

Preheat oven to 350 degrees.

Combine graham cracker crumbs, sugar, and melted butter in a bowl. Divide mixture evenly between the jars and lightly press crumb mixture into bottom of jars. Place in oven and bake for 5 minutes. Let cool.

Pour cream into sauce pan and add chocolate chips. Cook, over low heat until chocolate chips are melted. Stir often as chocolate is melting.

Divide up the chocolate mixture and spoon into the jars on top of the graham cracker crust. Top with 1/2 cup of mini marshmallows.

Place in preheated 400 degree oven for 12-15 until marshmallows are melted and turning golden brown.

Serve immediately and enjoy!

Frozen Lemonade Pie

• ▪ ▪ ▪ • ▪ ▪ ▪ • ▪ ▪ ▪ • ▪ ▪

This classic frozen lemonade pie works beautifully in a jar. This recipe uses 8-ounce jars, but if you want smaller portions just half the ingredients and use 4 ounce jars.

Servings: 8 8-ounce jars

Ingredients

1 1/2 cups graham cracker crumbs

1/3 cup sugar

6 tablespoons butter, melted

1 14-ounce can condensed milk

2 cups heavy cream

1 8-ounce can frozen lemonade concentrate, slightly thawed

Directions

Preheat oven to 350 degrees.

Combine graham cracker crumbs, sugar, and melted butter in a bowl. Divide mixture evenly between the jars and lightly press crumb mixture into bottom of jars. Place in oven and bake for 5 minutes. Let cool.

Whip the cream in a bowl until stiff. Add condensed milk and frozen lemonade concentrate. Gently fold together. Divide and pour mixture evenly into jars.

Seal jars and place in freezer at least 6 hours.

Peanut Butter Cups

Rich and delicious with a hidden peanut butter surprise.

Servings: 8 pint-size jars

Ingredients

4 ounces dark chocolate chips

11 tablespoons butter

2/3 cup fall-purpose flour

2 tablespoons cocoa powder

3/4 teaspoon baking powder

1 teaspoon salt

3/4 cup sugar

3 large eggs

1 teaspoon vanilla extract

1/2 cup peanut butter

1 cup chocolate fudge frosting

4 Reese's peanut butter cups, cut into pieces

Directions

In a microwave-safe bowl, add dark chocolate chips and butter (cut into pieces). Microwave until melted (check in 30 second intervals). Set aside.

In large bowl, combine flour, cocoa powder, baking powder, and salt. Whisk until blended. In a separate bowl, combine sugar, eggs, and vanilla. Beat together. Add in chocolate and butter mixture and blend. Fold in flour mixture and mix until blended. Do not overmix.

Distribute batter between the jars. Place jars on cookies sheet and bake in preheated 350 degree oven for 20-25 minutes or until toothpick comes out clean.

Cool slightly. Make hole in center of each jar. Spoon in 1 tablespoon of peanut butter.

Top with frosting and sprinkle with Reese's peanut butter cups.

Mini Apple Pies

• ▪ ▪ ▪ • ▪ ▪ ▪ • ▪ ▪ ▪ • ▪ ▪

These individual size pies can be baked right in the jar.

Servings: 4 half-pint jars

Ingredients

1 9-inch pie crust dough, premade or bought

2 cups apples, peeled and diced

2 tablespoons brown sugar

2 teaspoons cinnamon

1 teaspoon nutmeg

1 teaspoon vanilla

1 teaspoon lemon juice

2 tablespoons butter, melted

Sugar for sprinkling

Directions

Lay out the pie crust on a floured surface. Use the ring from one of the jars to cut 4 circles out of the dough. Set these aside for the tops.

Line each of the jars with dough. Press firmly against the sides of the jar.

In a bowl, mix apples, sugar, cinnamon, nutmeg, vanilla, and lemon juice.

Scoop 1/2 cup of apple filling into each jar.

Top each jar with pie crust top. Crimp edges and cut a slit in the top to vent.

Brush each pie with melted butter and sprinkle with sugar.

Place jars on cookie sheet and bake in preheated 400 degree oven for 40 minutes or until crust is golden brown.

Pies may also be frozen before baking. If baking from frozen, allow jar to come to room temperature before baking.

No-Bake Chocolate-Crusted Cheesecake

● ■ ● ■ ● ■ ● ■ ● ■ ● ■ ● ■ ● ■ ●

Strawberries, chocolate, and cheesecake—what more could you want in a dessert?

Servings: 4 pint-size jars

Ingredients

1 1/2 cups graham cracker crumbs

1/3 cup sugar

6 tablespoons butter, melted

2 tablespoons cocoa powder

1 quart strawberries, sliced

2 tablespoons sugar

1 cup whipped cream

1 8-ounce package of cream cheese, softened

1 14-ounce can condensed sweetened milk

juice of 1 lemon

1 tablespoon vanilla extract

Directions

Combine graham cracker crumbs, sugar, cocoa powder, and melted butter in a bowl. Divide mixture evenly between the jars and lightly press crumb mixture into bottom of jars.

Combine strawberries and sugar in a bowl. Mix to coat strawberries with sugar.

In a mixing bowl, combine cream cheese, condensed milk, lemon, and vanilla extract. Mix until smooth and fluffy.

Divide cream cheese filling and place 1/4 into jars. Top with strawberries and whipped cream.

Seal jars and chill in refrigerator until ready to serve.

Panna Cotta with Raspberry Sauce

Panna Cotta is an Italian custard-like dessert that is elegant yet easy to make.

Servings: 6 half-pint size jars

Ingredients

2 tablespoons water

1 1/2 teaspoons gelatin, unflavored

1 vanilla bean

2 cups whipping cream

1 1/2 cups plain yogurt, Greek-style

1 cup sugar, divided

2 12-ounce packages of frozen raspberries, thawed

Fresh raspberries for garnish

Directions

Mix together water and gelatin in a small bowl. Let sit for about 15 minutes..

Place raspberries in a bowl and stir in 1/2 cup sugar. Set aside.

In a large bowl, mix together 1 cup whipping cream with the yogurt.

In a small saucepan, pour remaining 1 cup cream and 1/2 cup sugar. Heat over medium heat. Split vanilla bean and add seeds and bean to pan. Stir until cream begins to simmer and the sugar is dissolved. Remove pan from heat and scoop out vanilla bean. Add gelatin to pan and stir to dissolve into cream. Add this mixture to bowl with cream and yogurt and stir until combined.

Divide cream mixture and raspberry sauce evenly between the six jars. Layer cream mixture followed by a layer of raspberry sauce. Repeat. Seal jar and store in refrigerator for at least three hours or overnight.

When ready to serve, top with fresh raspberries.

Vanilla Cupcakes in a Jar

* * * * * * * * * * * * * * * *

Simple, easy, and delicious! Perfect with a glass of cold milk.

Servings: 8 half-pint size jars

Ingredients

1 box vanilla cake mix

1 stick butter, salted, softened

8 ounces cream cheese, softened

4 cups confectioner's sugar

1 teaspoon vanilla extract

1 tablespoon heavy cream

Directions

Prepare cake mix according to package **Directions** and bake as directed in cupcake tins. Allow to cool.

For frosting, beat together butter and cream cheese with electric mixer until smooth. Add sugar, one cup at a time, vanilla extract, and cream. Beat until light and fluffy.

To assemble, slice cupcakes in half horizontally. Place one cupcake half in bottom of each jar.

Add a layer of frosting (using piping bag for easy filling). Add another cupcake half. Top with another layer of frosting.

Eat right away or seal jars and store in refrigerator. Cupcakes should stay fresh for 3-4 days.

Blueberry Parfaits

* ■ ■ ■ ● ■ ■ ■ ● ■ ■ ■ ● ■ ■

Make these ahead for a quick yet elegant dessert at your next dinner party.

Servings: 6 half-pint jars

Ingredients

1 1/2 cups graham cracker crumbs

1/3 cup sugar

6 tablespoons butter, melted

3 cups blueberries

3 cups sour cream

1 cup light brown sugar, lightly packed

2 tablespoons lemon juice

Whipped cream

Directions

Preheat oven to 350 degrees.

Combine graham cracker crumbs, sugar, and melted butter in a bowl. Divide mixture evenly between the jars and lightly press crumb mixture into bottom of jars. Place in oven and bake for 5 minutes. Let cool.

In a bowl, combine sour cream, sugar, and lemon juice.

Layer sour cream mixture, followed by layer of blueberries into jars. Repeat.

Top with whipped cream and a couple of blueberries.

Serve at once or seal jars and refrigerate until ready to eat.

Chocolate and Vanilla Cheesecake Jars

* ■ ■ ■ ■ ◆ ■ ■ ■ ◆ ■ ■ ◆ ■ ■

Chocolate graham cracker crust, creamy vanilla cheesecake, topped with rich chocolate ganache.

Servings: 8 half-pint jars

Ingredients

1 1/2 cups chocolate cookie crumbs

1/3 cup sugar

6 tablespoons butter, melted

1 8-ounce package of cream cheese, softened

1 14-ounce can condensed sweetened milk

juice of 1 lemon

1 tablespoon vanilla extract

1 cup heavy cream

1 1/2 cups chocolate chips, semi-sweet

Directions

Preheat oven to 350 degrees. Combine cookie crumbs, sugar, and melted butter in a bowl. Divide mixture evenly between the jars and lightly press crumb mixture into bottom of jars. Place on cookie sheet and bake for 10 minutes.

In a mixing bowl, combine cream cheese, condensed milk, lemon, and vanilla extract. Mix until smooth and fluffy.

In a saucepan over medium heat, add heavy cream and chocolate chips. Heat, stirring occasionally, until chips have melted.

Divide cream cheese filling and layer into jars. Spread chocolate mixture on top. Refrigerate for 3-4 hours before serving.

Raspberry Parfaits

Creamy, smooth, and delicious!

Servings: 4 pint-size jars

Ingredients

4 cups raspberries

1/4 cup sugar

1 cup ricotta cheese

4 ounces cream cheese, softened

1/4 cup powdered sugar

1 tablespoon water

1 teaspoon vanilla extract

Whipped cream for topping

Slivered almonds for topping (optional)

Directions

In a blender, place 2 cups raspberries and 1/4 cup sugar. Puree until smooth.

In a bowl, combine ricotta cheese, cream cheese, powdered sugar, water, and vanilla. Whisk until smooth.

Into each jar layer: cheese mixture, raspberry puree, 1/4 cup fresh raspberries. Repeat the layers. Refrigerate for 2 hours before serving.

Serve topped with whipped cream and slivered almonds.

Beverages

Mason jars are perfect for drinks, too!

Strawberry Lemonade Cocktail

Bright and sweet and perfect on a hot summer day.

Servings: 1 pint-size jar

Ingredients

1 1/2 ounces vodka

1 lemon wedge

2-3 strawberries

1 cup lemonade

1/2 cup ice

Directions

Add all ingredients to Mason jar. Seal jar and shake. Chill in refrigerator until ready to drink

Fresh-Squeezed Lemonade

Tart yet sweet—perfect when you want a small batch of fresh lemonade.

Servings: 1 quart-size jar

Ingredients

12 ounces water

1 lemon plus a couple of slices for garnish

1-2 tablespoons sugar, to desired sweetness

1/2 cup crushed ice

Directions

Cut lemon in half and squeeze juice and pulp into jar. Add water, sugar, and ice.

Close jar and shake well until sugar is dissolved. Open jar and add a couple of lemon slices for garnish.

Serve and enjoy!

Watermelon Margarita

This low-calorie cocktail is cool and refreshing

Servings: 6 half-pint jars

Ingredients

2 teaspoons sugar

3 1/2 cups watermelon, seedless and cubed

1/2 cup tequila

3 tablespoons lime juice

1 tablespoon Triple Sec

3 cups crushed ice

Kiwi slices for garnish

Directions

Add watermelon, tequila, lime juice, and Triple Sec to a blender. Blend until smooth.

Fill each Mason jar with 1/2 cup crushed ice. Add 1/2 cup margarita to each jar. Garnish with kiwi slice.

Serve and enjoy!

Lemon–Strawberry Fizzies

These drinks are cool, refreshing, and low-cal.

Servings: 1 pint-size jar

Ingredients

12 ounces sparkling water (La Croix, Pellegrino, etc.)

4-5 strawberries

1 tablespoon lemon juice

2-3 lemon slices

1-2 mint leaves

Ice

Directions

Puree the strawberries in a blender.

Add all ingredients to jar. Seal jar and shake well.

Enjoy!

Note: The variations with this recipe are virtually endless. You could substitute the strawberries with blueberries, raspberries, melon, or orange.

Cherry Peach Sangria

Delicious, fruity sangria that's perfect for a special occasion.

Servings: 1 quart-size jar

Ingredients

1/8 cup sugar

1/8 cup brandy

1 cup pitted Rainier cherries

1/2 bottle white wine

1/2 cup club soda

1/2 peach, sliced

Mint leaves for garnish

Directions

Combine sugar and brandy in jar, stirring until sugar dissolves. Add cherries and wine and chill for several hours or overnight.

Before serving add chilled club soda, peaches, and garnish.

Blueberry Smoothie

Did you know your Mason jar can fit right on the blender? Give it a try and blend this smoothie right in the jar for an easy to clean up treat.

Servings: 1 pint size jar

Ingredients

1/2 cup blueberries, fresh or frozen

4 ounces plain yogurt

1/3 cup milk (cow, soy, almond)

1 tablespoon sugar

1/2 teaspoon vanilla extract

Directions

To make this smoothie right in the jar, you will need to use a regular mouth (not wide mouth) jar.

Put all ingredients into jar. Unscrew the base from your blender's pitcher and attach it to the Mason jar. Fit onto blender and blend until smooth.

Unscrew blender blade and you are ready to drink.

Mojitos

Mint, lime, rum, yum!

Servings: 1 pint-size jar

Ingredients

1 1/2 ounces white rum

1/2 lime, cut into 4 wedges

2 tablespoons sugar

8-10 mint leaves

1/2 cup club soda

1 cup ice, crushed

Directions

Place mint leaves, 3 lime wedges, and sugar into bottom of jar. Use muddler to crush mint and limes, do not over muddle.

Add ice, rum, and soda water. Seal jar and shake.

Enjoy!

Dressings

Sweet Citrus Dressing

Use this dressing with the Rainbow Fruit Salad.

Servings: 4

Ingredients

1/2 cup orange juice

juice of 1 lemon (around 4 tablespoons)

2 tablespoons honey

1/2 teaspoon grated ginger (or ground)

Directions

Whisk together all ingredients in a bowl until well blended.

Balsamic Vinaigrette Dressing

This all-purpose dressing works with most green salads.

Servings: 4

Ingredients

1/4 cup extra-virgin olive oil

2 tablespoons balsamic vinegar

1 teaspoon Dijon mustard

1/2 teaspoon sugar or honey

1 clove garlic, minced

1/2 shallot, minced

Black pepper, freshly ground, to taste

Directions

Whisk together all ingredients in a bowl until well blended. Use immediately or store in glass jar with lid in refrigerator.

Caesar Vinaigrette Dressing

This dressing is perfect with pasta salad.

Servings: 4

Ingredients

1/3 cup extra-virgin olive oil

3 tablespoons apple cider vinegar

1/2 teaspoon sugar

1/4 cup grated Romano cheese

1 clove garlic, minced

Directions

Whisk together all ingredients in a bowl until well blended. Use immediately or store in glass jar with lid in refrigerator.

Greek Dressing

Perfect paired with Greek Salad.

Servings: 4

Ingredients

1/2 cup olive oil

1/2 red wine vinegar

1 tablespoon Dijon mustard

1 clove garlic, minced

1 teaspoon dried oregano

1 teaspoon dried basil

Salt and pepper to taste

Directions

Whisk together all ingredients in a bowl until well blended. Use immediately or store in glass jar with lid in refrigerator.

Honey Mustard Vinaigrette

A little bit sweet, a little bit tangy.

Servings: 4

Ingredients

1/2 cup extra-virgin olive oil

1/4 cup apple cider vinegar

1/2 tablespoon dijon mustard

1/2 tablespoon honey

Salt and pepper to taste

Directions

Whisk together all ingredients in a bowl until well blended. Use immediately or store in glass jar with lid in refrigerator.

Raspberry Vinaigrette Dressing

Servings: 6

Ingredients

1/2 cup extra-virgin olive oil

1/2 cup raspberry wine vinegar

2 teaspoons Dijon mustard

1 teaspoon sugar

Salt and pepper to taste

Directions

Whisk together all ingredients in a bowl until well blended. Use immediately or store in glass jar with lid in refrigerator.

Poppy Seed Dressing

I like this dressing with both fruit salad and chicken salad.

Servings: 6

Ingredients

1/2 olive oil

1/4 cup white wine vinegar

1 teaspoon Dijon mustard

2 teaspoons sugar

1 tablespoon poppy seeds

Salt and pepper to taste

Directions

Whisk together all ingredients in a bowl until well blended. Use immediately or store in glass jar with lid in refrigerator.

White Wine Vinaigrette Dressing

Servings: 6

Ingredients

1/2 cup extra-virgin olive oil

1/4 cup white wine vinegar

1 teaspoon sugar

1 garlic clove, minced

Salt and pepper to taste

Directions

Whisk together all ingredients in a bowl until well blended. Use immediately or store in glass jar with lid in refrigerator.

Lemony Yogurt Dressing

Try this when you're in the mood for a creamy dressing.

Servings: 6

Ingredients

1 cup plain Greek-style yogurt

2 tablespoons extra-virgin olive oil

Juice of 1 lemon

2 garlic cloves, minced

Salt and pepper to taste

Directions

Add all ingredients to blender. Blend on low setting until combined.

Store in refrigerator until ready to use.

Index

From the Author

Thank you for reading *Mason Jar Meals: Delicious and Easy Jar Salads, Jar Lunches, and More for Meals on the Go.* I sincerely hope that you found this book informative and helpful.

It would be greatly appreciated if you could take a few moments to share your opinion and post a review for this book on Amazon or other retailer where you purchased this book. Your positive review helps us to reach other readers and provides valuable feedback with which we can improve future books.

Thank you!

Made in the USA
Lexington, KY
29 September 2015